Darknet

Expert Guide to Online Anonymity and Digital Secrecy

Ryan Knight

Dedication

To the curious souls who peek beyond the surface, To the daydreamers who build castles in code, To the everyday heroes whispering secrets in encrypted chats, This book is your secret handshake in the digital dance.

No matter if you're a seasoned shadow explorer or just taking your first steps, these pages hold your key to online freedom. They'll teach you tricks to vanish, tools to outsmart the trackers, and the confidence to own your digital destiny.

So grab your flashlight and dive into the hidden corners of the web. Together, we'll rewrite the rules and reclaim the shadows as our playground.

Remember, privacy isn't about hiding, it's about choosing how you shine. Go forth, light your spark, and let the shadows dance!

About the Author

Ryan Knight isn't your typical security expert. His expertise was forged not in boardrooms, but in the shadowy corners of the internet, where he honed his skills as a hacker and trainer for the FBI and NSA.

His passion for online anonymity isn't about secrecy for its own sake, but about empowering individuals to reclaim their digital sovereignty in an age of surveillance.

In "Darknet: Expert Guide to Online Anonymity and Digital Secrecy," Ryan invites you on a thrilling journey through the darknet's hidden pathways, arming you with the knowledge to protect your privacy, explore its potential, and navigate its challenges with confidence.

Join him. Unmask the secrets of the shadows, master the tools of anonymity, and reclaim your rightful place as a free and empowered citizen of the digital world.

Table of Contents

Chapter 1:

Why Privacy Matters

Imagine a world where every whispered word, every fleeting thought, every click and keystroke is laid bare. Not just to the NSA or some faceless corporation, but to anyone – your neighbor, your boss, your ex. A world where privacy isn't a right, but a luxury reserved for the tech elite and the deeply paranoid. Welcome to the precipice of that world, to the edge of the looking glass into a future increasingly defined by a lack of privacy.

This isn't some dystopian novel; it's the reality we're sleepwalking into. Governments hungry for control collect our data without a blink, corporations monetize our every move, and hackers lurk in the shadows, ready to exploit any vulnerability. Our digital footprints paint an intimate portrait of who we are – our desires, our fears, our secrets – laid bare for anyone with the right tools or enough rubles.

But within this chilling reality lies a flicker of defiance, a rebellion against the panoptic gaze. It's called privacy, and in the labyrinthine underbelly of the internet, it has a name: the Darknet. It's a place where shadows dance and anonymity reigns, where you can shed your digital skin and step into a world free from the prying eyes of the state, the corporations, and the voyeurs.

So, why should you care about privacy? It's not just about hiding your browsing history from your mother-in-law (though that can be handy). It's about protecting your freedom of expression, your right to dissent, your very ability to be an individual in a world increasingly obsessed with categorization and control.

Imagine speaking your mind on a controversial topic without fear of reprisal. Imagine exploring unpopular ideas without being labeled an extremist. Imagine pursuing your passions, both online and offline, without your every move being tracked and monetized. This is the promise of privacy, the potential for a world where your thoughts and actions belong to you, and only you.

But to truly understand the importance of privacy, we need to understand the threats that loom.

The Ghost in the Machine: The Threats to Privacy

Governments: From mass surveillance programs to data retention laws, governments are increasingly turning into digital Big Brothers, watching our every move and collecting our most intimate information. The line between national security and individual liberty blurs ever finer, leaving citizens at the mercy of algorithms and opaque bureaucracies.

Corporations: Driven by the insatiable hunger for data, corporations mine our online lives for every nugget of information they can. Our browsing habits, our social media posts, our location data – it's all grist for the mill, turned into targeted advertising and manipulative algorithms. They know us better than we know ourselves, and they use that knowledge to influence our choices, sell us things we don't need, and manipulate our behavior.

Hackers: Lurking in the shadows of the digital world, hackers are the opportunistic predators of the online jungle. They exploit vulnerabilities in software and systems, steal our data, and hold it hostage for ransom. Our financial information, our medical records, our very identities – all are up for grabs in the hands of a skilled hacker.

Is there hope?

In the face of these threats, it's easy to fall into despair. But that's where the Darknet comes in. It's not a panacea, but it's a powerful tool for reclaiming your privacy, a weapon against the digital panopticon. In the following chapters, we'll delve into the intricacies of the Darknet, explore its tools and techniques, and equip you with the knowledge and skills to navigate this hidden world safely and effectively.

This is not just a book about technology; it's a call to action. It's a call to reclaim your right to privacy, to protect your freedom of expression, and to carve out a space in the digital world where you can be yourself, without fear or judgment.

Chapter 2:

The Building Blocks of Anonymity

In the last chapter, we explored the chilling reality of our shrinking digital privacy and the potential of the Darknet to fight back. Now, it's time to roll up our sleeves and learn the key tools we'll use to build our very own fortress of anonymity. Think of it like constructing a secret hideout, but instead of bricks and mortar, we'll use virtual building blocks like encryption, pseudonymity, and that legendary guardian of online shadows – Tor.

First Base: Encryption – Sealing the Secrets Away

Imagine sending a postcard written in a language only you and the recipient understand. That's essentially what encryption does with your data. It scrambles your information into a jumbled mess, like a locked treasure chest, using complex algorithms that require a special key to unlock. This key becomes the password to your digital secrets, ensuring only authorized eyes can decipher them.

Think of email or online banking. When you log in with a password, an encryption handshake happens, making sure your info travels securely between your device and the website. Pretty cool, right? But encryption comes in different flavors, each with its own strengths and quirks.

- Symmetric Encryption: Think of it as a single key for both locking and unlocking the treasure chest. It's efficient for quick exchanges, but if someone gets hold of that key, all your secrets are out in the open.

- Asymmetric Encryption: This is like having two keys – a public key everyone can see (like the lock on the chest) and a private key kept hidden under your mattress (the key to unlock it). You share the public key with anyone who needs to send you encrypted messages, but only you have the private key to decrypt them, making it much more secure.

Second Base: Pseudonymity – Wearing a Digital Mask

Imagine walking into a party with a cool alias and a killer disguise. Pseudonymity works the same way online. You shed your real name and use a fake one, like a pseudonym author using a pen name. This protects your real identity while still allowing you to interact online. Think of forums and online communities where you can choose a username and express yourself without revealing your full name.

But don't get too comfortable. While pseudonymity makes you harder to track, it's not foolproof. If you link your pseudonym to your real-world identity through emails or social media, your mask can slip.

The Big Gun: Tor – The Labyrinthine Defender

Now, picture yourself navigating a city through a network of secret tunnels and passageways, each one leading to another, making it impossible for anyone to track your path. That's Tor in a nutshell. It's a free software that bounces your internet traffic through multiple relays around the world, making it almost impossible to pinpoint your location or origin. Think of it as the ultimate shield against online snooping.

Tor is powerful, but like any tool, it's not perfect. It can be slower than regular browsing, and some websites might block it. But for serious anonymity seekers, Tor is a must-have in their privacy toolkit.

Building Your Privacy Toolkit: Mixing and Matching for Maximum Protection

Remember, the best defense is a layered one. Just like mixing spices enhances the flavor of a dish, combining different anonymity tools can significantly boost your online stealth. Here's a basic toolkit to get you started:

- A strong password manager: Generate and store unique passwords for each website you use, making it harder for hackers to crack a single password and access all your accounts.

- A privacy-focused browser: Consider options like Firefox and Brave that prioritize user privacy over data collection.

- Encryption software: Encrypt your sensitive files and folders to keep them safe from prying eyes even if your device is compromised.

- Tor: For venturing into the Darknet or when extra anonymity is needed.

Remember, your privacy toolkit is unique to you and your needs. As you gain confidence and knowledge, you can experiment and add more tools to your arsenal. Just keep in mind that while anonymity is powerful, it's not magic. Responsible online behavior and a healthy dose of paranoia are always your best allies.

Now, with these foundation blocks in place, we're ready to delve deeper into the fascinating world of the Darknet in the next chapter. Get ready to put on your digital cloak and hood – the adventure awaits!

Chapter 3:

Tor: The King of Anonymity Networks

Tor, the king of anonymity networks, isn't a single entity, but a sprawling ecosystem buzzing with interconnected parts. Understanding how these elements work together is crucial for navigating this labyrinthine path to online privacy. So, grab your digital compass and join us as we delve into the fascinating world of the Tor ecosystem.

The Architects: Tor Relays - Pillars of the Labyrinth

Imagine a hidden network of relay stations, each one dedicated to obscuring your digital trail. These are the Tor relays, the lifeblood of the ecosystem. These volunteer-run computers receive your encrypted data, strip away a layer of encryption, and send it on to another random relay in the network. This multi-hop dance continues until your data reaches its final destination, effectively erasing your footprints along the way.

To visualize this, picture yourself sending a letter cloaked in multiple envelopes. Each relay removes one envelope, revealing an address for the next relay, further masking your original location. By the time the final envelope reaches its recipient, your trail is cold, your location shrouded in the vastness of the network.

Types of Tor Relays:

- Entry Guards: The first stop on your Tor journey, these relays act as trusted entry points into the network.

- Middle Relays: The backbone of the ecosystem, these relays handle the bulk of data traffic, forwarding it through the labyrinth.

- Exit Nodes: The final stop before your data reaches its destination, these relays are responsible for decrypting the last layer and sending it out into the clearnet (the regular internet).

Downloading and Setting Up Tor:

Ready to join the Tor ecosystem? The journey begins with the Tor Browser Bundle, available for download on their official website: https://www.torproject.org/download/. This bundle comes pre-configured with everything you need to navigate the Tor network, including the Tor Browser itself. Installation is straightforward, and getting started is as simple as launching the browser and connecting to the network.

Unmasking the Gatekeepers: Exit Nodes - The Final Frontier

After traversing the labyrinthine Tor network, your data reaches its final destination through an exit node. Think of it as the doorway back to the clearnet, the point where your data emerges from the shadows. While the relays have stripped away your identifying information, the exit node plays a crucial role in the anonymity equation.

Choosing Your Guardians Wisely:

The choice of exit node impacts your security and experience. Ideally, you want one that:

- Resides in a privacy-friendly jurisdiction: Choose nodes located in countries with strong data protection laws and minimal government surveillance.

- Has a good reputation: Opt for well-established nodes with reliable uptime and minimal malicious activity reported.

- Matches your needs: Some nodes may be optimized for speed, while others prioritize security or censorship circumvention. Choose based on your individual needs.

The Shadow Side of the Gateway:

Despite their importance, exit nodes pose a potential vulnerability. Since they decrypt the final layer of your data and send it to the clearnet, they have the technical capability to eavesdrop on your traffic. To mitigate this risk:

- Use HTTPS wherever possible: Encrypting your communication adds an extra layer of protection on top of Tor's anonymity.

- Be mindful of what you do on Tor: While Tor helps mask your identity, it doesn't make you invincible. Avoid sensitive activities like online banking or sharing confidential information on exit nodes.

The Price of Privacy: Risks and Limitations of Using Tor

Like any powerful tool, Tor comes with its own set of limitations and potential risks. Understanding these caveats is crucial for making informed decisions about your online anonymity journey.

Speed Bumps on the Labyrinthine Path:

Tor's multi-hop architecture naturally impacts your internet speed. Data takes longer to traverse the network, resulting in slower browsing and download times. Patience is key if you choose to embrace the Tor ecosystem.

Exit Node Vulnerability: As mentioned earlier, exit nodes pose a potential security risk. Choosing trustworthy nodes and practicing responsible online behavior are essential to minimizing this risk.

Government Scrutiny: The association of Tor with certain online activities attracts scrutiny from some governments. While not illegal in itself, be aware of potential restrictions or monitoring in your region.

Legal Gray Areas: Certain activities on Tor, like accessing illegal markets or engaging in hacking, are illegal. Remember, anonymity isn't a license to break the law.

Beyond the Technical Hurdles:

Using Tor can require a slight shift in your online habits. Websites may load slower, some may not work at all, and accessing certain services might be more challenging. But remember, the trade-off is increased privacy and online freedom.

Joining the Labyrinthine Community: Exploring the Tor Ecosystem

While the anonymity Tor offers can be a solitary journey, it's far from a lonely one. The Tor ecosystem boasts a vibrant and diverse community of individuals drawn together by a shared desire for online freedom and privacy.

This community offers invaluable support, resources, and a sense of belonging for those navigating the labyrinthine paths of the network.

Forums and Hidden Wikis:

Dive into the bustling Tor forums, where users share tips, troubleshoot issues, and discuss the latest developments in the ecosystem. Hidden wikis, accessible only through Tor, offer a wealth of information on everything from choosing exit nodes to finding hidden services (websites accessible only through Tor).

Mailing Lists and IRC Channels:

Engage in real-time conversations on Tor-specific mailing lists and IRC channels. These platforms foster a sense of community, allowing you to connect with like-minded individuals, ask questions, and learn from experienced users.

Events and Conferences:

Venture beyond the digital realm and attend Tor-related conferences and workshops happening around the world. These events provide opportunities to network with fellow enthusiasts, learn from experts, and contribute to the ongoing development of the ecosystem.

Contributing to the Cause:

The Tor Project relies on the dedication of volunteers to maintain and improve the network. Whether it's offering technical expertise, translating documentation, or simply spreading awareness, there are numerous ways to contribute to the cause and strengthen the community.

Remember, the Tor ecosystem is more than just a network; it's a movement. It's a community of individuals united by a common goal: protecting online privacy and promoting digital freedom. By joining the conversation, sharing your knowledge, and contributing to the cause, you become an integral part of this movement, ensuring the continued existence of this vital labyrinth of anonymity for generations to come.

So, are you ready to take the plunge? Download the Tor Browser, explore the resources, and join the labyrinthine community. The journey towards online privacy awaits.

Additional Resources:

- Tor Project
  website: https://www.torproject.org/

- Tor Blog: https://blog.torproject.org/

- Tor
  Forum: https://forum.torproject.org/

- The Hidden
  Wiki: http://b7zq5i7zftu5y73pw.onion/

- Tor IRC channel: #tor on Libera.Chat

With this chapter concluded, we've shed light on the inner workings of the Tor network, its strengths and limitations, and the vibrant community that sustains it. Remember, the journey to online privacy is a continuous one, and the Tor ecosystem offers a powerful tool for navigating the labyrinthine paths towards a more secure and free internet. Now, with knowledge as your guide and community at your side, venture forth and explore the depths of the Darknet, always remembering to tread cautiously and responsibly.

Chapter 4:

Beyond Tor: Alternative Anonymity Networks

While Tor reigns supreme as the king of anonymity networks, its labyrinthine paths aren't for everyone. In this chapter, we'll set sail for uncharted waters and explore alternative anonymity networks like I2P and Zcash, each offering unique features and trade-offs. So, fasten your digital life vests and prepare to dive into the depths of online privacy beyond the Tor horizon.

I2P: Building Your Own Island of Anonymity

Imagine not just navigating a labyrinth, but building your own hidden island within it. That's the essence of I2P (Invisible Internet Project), a peer-to-peer network where users directly connect with each other, eliminating the need for centralized servers. This unique architecture offers several advantages:

- Enhanced Security: With no central points of failure, I2P is inherently more resistant to attack and surveillance.

- Greater Control: Users have significant control over their anonymity, customizing their connections and network settings.

- Censorship Resistance: I2P is highly resistant to censorship and blocking attempts, making it a valuable tool in restrictive environments.

However, this island paradise comes with its own quirks:

- Steeper Learning Curve: Setting up and using I2P can be technically demanding, requiring more effort than the user-friendly Tor Browser.

- Slower Network: The peer-to-peer nature of I2P typically leads to slower speeds compared to Tor, making it less suitable for bandwidth-intensive activities.

- Limited Ecosystem: The I2P network is smaller than Tor, offering a narrower range of applications and services.

Zcash: Cloaking Your Coins in Secrecy

While Tor hides your online footprints, it doesn't mask your financial transactions. Enter Zcash, a privacy-focused cryptocurrency leveraging cutting-edge cryptography to shield your financial movements from prying eyes. Zcash boasts several unique features:

- Selective Transparency: Transactions can be either transparent or shielded, offering flexibility and control over your privacy needs.

- Enhanced Fungibility: All Zcash coins are indistinguishable, preventing tracking and analysis of individual transactions.

- Stronger Security: Zcash utilizes advanced cryptographic techniques, making it resistant to sophisticated hacking attempts.

However, the shiny Zcash coin also has its tarnished corners:

- Complexity and Uncertainty: Zcash's underlying cryptography is complex and not fully understood, raising concerns about potential vulnerabilities.

- Regulatory Scrutiny: As a privacy-focused cryptocurrency, Zcash attracts scrutiny from governments and financial institutions, potentially limiting its widespread adoption.

- Limited Integration: Compared to more established cryptocurrencies, Zcash has a smaller merchant and exchange network, reducing its practical use cases.

Choosing the Right Network: Mapping Your Anonymity Journey

So, which network should you choose? The answer, like all things in life, depends on your individual needs and priorities. Here's a handy compass to guide you:

- For the Privacy Purist: If anonymity is your paramount concern, and you're comfortable with technical complexity, I2P's decentralized architecture might be your haven.

- For the Tech-Savvy Financier: If financial privacy is your primary goal, and you're willing to navigate the uncharted waters of cryptography, Zcash could be your digital fortress.

- For the Everyday User: For most users seeking robust anonymity without deep technical dives, Tor remains the tried-and-true option, offering user-friendliness and a vibrant ecosystem.

Remember, the perfect anonymity network doesn't exist. Each option comes with its own set of strengths and weaknesses, making it crucial to understand your needs and choose the tool that best aligns with your personal digital journey. Explore, experiment, and stay informed! With knowledge as your compass and caution as your rudder, you can navigate the diverse seas of anonymity, charting your own course towards a more private and secure digital future.

Here are links and steps to get started with each of the anonymity networks discussed:

I2P

- Official Website: https://geti2p.net/en/

- Getting Started
  Guide: https://geti2p.net/en/download

- Key Steps:

    1. Download and install the I2P
       software from the official website.

    2. Run the I2P router application.

    3. Configure your web browser to
       use I2P (instructions provided in
       the getting started guide).

    4. Access I2P-specific websites and
       services through your configured
       browser.

Zcash

- Official Website: https://z.cash/

- Getting Started
  Guide: https://z.cash/get-started/

- Key Steps:

1. Create a Zcash wallet (either a standalone wallet or one integrated with an exchange).

2. Obtain Zcash coins through exchange platforms or mining.

3. Use your wallet to send and receive Zcash privately.

Tor

- Official Website: https://www.torproject.org/

- Download Tor Browser: https://www.torproject.org/download/

- Key Steps:

  1. Download and install the Tor Browser Bundle from the official website.

  2. Run the Tor Browser.

3. Access websites through the Tor network by simply browsing as you normally would.

Additional Tips for Using Anonymity Networks:

- Stay informed: Keep up-to-date with the latest news and developments related to each network.

- Use reputable services: Only access websites and services that are known to be trustworthy and secure.

- Practice good security hygiene: Use strong passwords, enable two-factor authentication, and be cautious about the information you share online.

- Respect the law: Remember that anonymity networks do not exempt you from legal obligations. Use them responsibly and ethically.

This chapter concludes our exploration of the captivating world of anonymity networks. We've ventured beyond the familiar shores of Tor, discovering the unique landscapes of I2P and Zcash, and equipped you with the tools to choose the network that best fits your needs. Remember, the quest for online privacy is an ongoing adventure, and the diverse tools at your disposal empower you to reclaim your digital freedom, one anonymous step at a time.

Chapter 5:

Securing Your Communications: Email, Messaging, and More

In the digital age, every message you send, every call you make, leaves a trail in the ether. But fear not, privacy warrior! This chapter equips you with the tools and tactics to turn your communications into hushed whispers, shielding them from prying ears and curious eyes. We'll dive into anonymizing your email, instant messaging, and even phone calls, weaving your own cloak of digital secrecy.

Email: From Open Postcards to Encrypted Missives

Imagine sending your emails not on flimsy postcards, but in locked metal boxes, delivered by trusted couriers. That's essentially what encrypted email does. Here are your options:

- End-to-End Encryption (E2EE) Services: Services like ProtonMail, Tutanota, and StartMail offer E2EE for your emails, ensuring only the sender and recipient can access the content.

- PGP (Pretty Good Privacy) Encryption: For the tech-savvy, PGP provides another layer of encryption, allowing you to secure emails sent to any recipient, even those not using E2EE services.

Instant Messaging: From Public Square to Hidden Alleyways

Leaving your conversations exposed in public squares like Facebook Messenger or WhatsApp isn't ideal. Fortunately, there are more secluded alleyways of the digital world:

- Signal: This widely used app boasts E2EE messaging, disappearing messages, and screenshot blocking, making it a haven for confidential chats.

- Telegram: While not E2EE by default, Telegram's "Secret Chats" offer E2EE and self-destructing messages, ideal for sensitive conversations.

- Wickr Me: This ephemeral messaging app disappears messages after a set time, ensuring complete privacy and zero digital footprints.

Phone Calls: From Open Lines to Encrypted Tunnels

- Signal Private Messenger: Not just for messaging, Signal also offers secure voice calls with E2EE encryption.

- Silent Circle: This subscription-based service provides E2EE voice calls, messaging, and video conferencing for business-level security.

- Jitsi Meet: For open-source enthusiasts, Jitsi Meet offers browser-based, E2EE-encrypted video conferencing without the need for downloads or installations.

Best Practices for Secure Communication:

Now that you have your digital cloak and dagger, here are some essential practices to maintain your communication security:

- Choose strong passwords and enable two-factor authentication (2FA) for all your accounts.

- Be cautious about what information you share online, especially with unfamiliar individuals.

- Avoid using public Wi-Fi for sensitive communication.

- Remember, no security is foolproof. Be vigilant and adapt your techniques based on your threat level.

Embracing a Culture of Privacy

Securing your communication isn't just about shielding individual messages; it's about cultivating a culture of privacy in your digital life. By taking conscious steps to control your data and safeguard your conversations, you reclaim your right to a private space in the online world. Remember, your whispers deserve to be heard only by those you choose, not the digital eavesdroppers lurking in the shadows.

With this chapter, we've demystified the world of secure communication, equipping you with the tools and tactics to cloak your words in a shroud of digital secrecy. As you navigate the ever-evolving landscape of online privacy, remember that your dedication to secure communication is a small flame flickering against the darkness, paving the way for a future where whispers can carry freely, unburdened by fear and unfettered by intrusive eyes. Keep whispering, dear reader, and together we'll make sure our voices are heard, loud and clear, within the hushed chambers of digital privacy.

This concludes our exploration of the essential tools and techniques for navigating the Darknet and beyond. From understanding hidden networks to securing your communications, you're now equipped to venture deeper into the labyrinthine alleys of online anonymity, safeguarding your freedom and privacy in the digital age. Remember, knowledge is your shield, caution is your compass, and responsibility is your torch. Embrace the shadows, wield your tools wisely, and keep exploring the hidden corners of the internet where your true voice can still be heard.

Chapter 6:

Browsing the Web Anonymously

Surfing the web, once a carefree joyride, has become a minefield of trackers, surveillance, and targeted ads. But fear not, digital pirates! This chapter equips you with the tools and tactics to navigate the stormy seas of online anonymity, becoming a ghost ship gliding unseen under the digital radar. We'll dive into the two main anchors of anonymous browsing – Tor and VPNs – exploring their strengths, weaknesses, and how to choose the right one for your unique needs.

Tor: The Labyrinthine Cloak of Anonymity

Imagine your internet traffic meandering through a maze of encrypted tunnels, bouncing off countless relays before reaching its destination. That's the magic of Tor, the anonymity network weaving a cloak of obscurity around your browsing habits. Here's what it offers:

- Strong Anonymity: Tor's multi-hop architecture makes it incredibly difficult to track your online movements, keeping your browsing history and location shrouded in secrecy.

- Censorship Circumvention: Tor bypasses geographical restrictions and firewalls, letting you access blocked websites and information freely.

- Privacy Protection: Tor shields your data from snoopers, prying eyes, and malicious actors, safeguarding your online identity.

But even the Labyrinthine King has its limitations:

- Speed Bumps: The multi-hop journey comes at a cost – slower internet speeds are the price for your digital invisibility.

- Exit Node Vulnerability: While your data is encrypted within the Tor network, the final exit node can potentially see your unencrypted traffic.

- Technical Complexity: Setting up and using Tor requires more technical expertise than using a simple browser.

VPNs: Tunneling Through the Digital Landscape

Imagine yourself driving through a secure tunnel, shielded from prying eyes on the open road. That's essentially what a VPN (Virtual Private Network) does – it encrypts your internet traffic and routes it through a remote server, masking your true location and identity. Here are its benefits:

- Location Masking: VPNs change your virtual location, letting you access geo-restricted content and bypass censorship.

- Enhanced Security: Encryption protects your data from prying eyes on public Wi-Fi networks and untrusted connections.

- Privacy Boost: VPNs hide your IP address, making it harder for websites and online services to track your online activity.

However, the VPN tunnel also has its tollbooths:

- Subscription Costs: Most reliable VPNs require paid subscriptions, adding a financial cost to your anonymity.

- Performance Impact: Depending on the server location and your internet connection, VPNs can also slow down your internet speed.

- Trust Factor: Choosing a trustworthy VPN provider is crucial, as they handle your encrypted data.

Choosing Your Vessel: Tor vs. VPN – A Captain's Dilemma

So, which digital vessel should you set sail with? The answer, like most things in life, depends on your needs and priorities:

- For Ultimate Anonymity: Tor reigns supreme, especially for bypassing censorship and protecting against advanced tracking.

- For Convenience and Location Masking: VPNs offer ease of use and location flexibility, ideal for everyday browsing and accessing geo-restricted content.

- For a Balanced Approach: Combining Tor with a VPN provides ultimate security, but at the cost of slower speeds and technical complexity.

Remember, no single tool is perfect. Assess your threat level, browsing habits, and technical aptitude to choose the right balance of anonymity and convenience.

Beyond the Tools: Sailing With Caution

Regardless of your chosen vessel, remember:

- Choose trustworthy tools: Do your research and select reputable Tor relays and VPN providers.

- Practice good online hygiene: Use strong passwords, avoid suspicious websites, and be mindful of the information you share online.

- Stay informed: Keep up-to-date with the latest developments in the world of online privacy and security.

Embracing the Ghostly Life

Browsing anonymously isn't just about hiding your online tracks; it's about reclaiming your digital freedom. By wielding the tools and tactics in this chapter, you transform from a tracked and targeted user into a digital ghost, invisible to the prying eyes of the online world. So, raise your anonymized sails, captain, and chart your course toward a more private and secure internet experience. Remember, the open seas beckon, and the shadows of the digital labyrinth wait for you to explore their hidden depths.

This concludes our exploration of the essential tools and tactics for navigating the Darknet and beyond. From understanding hidden networks to securing your communications and browsing anonymously, you're now equipped to venture deeper into the labyrinthine alleys of online anonymity, safeguarding your freedom and privacy in the digital age. Remember, knowledge is your shield, caution is your compass.

Here are some links to get started with the tools and resources discussed in Chapter 6:

Tor:

- Official Website: https://www.torproject.org/

- Download Tor Browser: https://www.torproject.org/download/

- Tor Documentation: https://tb-manual.torproject.org/

VPNs:

- Independent VPN Review Sites:

    o https://www.trustpilot.com/review/vpnmentor.com

- https://www.top10vpn.com/

- https://www.privacyguides.org/en/basics/vpn-overview/

- Popular VPN Providers:

  - NordVPN: https://nordvpn.com/

  - ExpressVPN: https://www.expressvpn.com/

  - ProtonVPN: https://protonvpn.com/

Additional Resources:

- Electronic Frontier Foundation (EFF): https://www.eff.org/

- Privacy International: https://privacyinternational.org/

- Digital Shadows: https://www.reliaquest.com/platform/digital-risk-protection/

Choosing the Right Tool:

- Tor vs. VPN Comparison
  Chart: https://www.elite-proxy.net/vpn-vs-tor-whats-the-difference-for-online-privacy-and-anonymity/

- Privacy Tools & Services
  Directory: https://www.privacytools.io/

Remember, the best approach to online anonymity often involves combining multiple tools and techniques. Research your options, choose what works best for your needs, and stay vigilant about your online security practices.

I hope these resources help you navigate the shadows of the digital sea with confidence!

Chapter 7:

Anonymity on the Go: Mobile Devices and Tor

The digital revolution has placed the internet in our pockets, but with it comes the constant shadow of surveillance and data collection. But fear not, intrepid mobile voyagers! This chapter equips you with the tools and tactics to transform your smartphone into a phantom vessel, sailing the seas of online anonymity while leaving barely a ripple in your wake. We'll dive into the challenges and solutions for using Tor and other anonymity tools on your mobile devices, empowering you to reclaim your digital freedom on the go.

Tor in Your Pocket: Weaving a Mobile Web of Secrecy

The mighty Tor Browser isn't confined to desktops; it boasts mobile versions for both

Android and iOS, letting you cloak your mobile browsing in its labyrinthine layers of anonymity. Here's what you need to know:

- Tor Browser for Android: The official and recommended option, offering strong anonymity and a familiar Tor experience.

- Onion Browser for iOS: Due to Apple's restrictions, Onion Browser relies on iOS's built-in web engine, limiting Tor's full features but still providing basic anonymity.

Navigating the Mobile Labyrinth: Challenges and Solutions

While Tor unlocks mobile anonymity, the path isn't without its bumps:

- Battery Drain: Tor's multi-hop connections can significantly drain your battery, necessitating a portable charger if venturing far from an outlet.

- Performance Impact: Expect slower browsing speeds when using Tor on mobile, especially compared to your usual data connection.

- Limited Ecosystem: Not all websites or apps are accessible through Tor on mobile, requiring extra caution and potentially limiting your options.

Overcoming the Obstacles: Tips for Mobile Anonymity

Embrace these tactics to smooth your anonymous mobile journey:

- Pre-download essential resources: Save offline copies of crucial websites or documents to minimize reliance on live Tor browsing.

- Utilize Wi-Fi for heavier tasks: Reserve bandwidth-intensive activities like streaming or video calls for regular internet connections.

- Stay informed: Keep up-to-date with the latest Tor mobile developments and adjust your tactics accordingly.

Beyond Tor: Additional Mobile Anonymity Tools

While Tor stands tall, your mobile anonymity arsenal can benefit from other tools:

- VPNs: Offer location masking and additional encryption, but can be resource-intensive and often require subscriptions.

- Privacy-focused Browsers: Alternatives like DuckDuckGo and Firefox Focus offer basic privacy features without the full Tor experience.

- Messaging Apps: Signal and Telegram provide secure messaging with additional privacy features like disappearing messages.

Embracing the Mobile Ghost: A Call to Action

Mobile anonymity isn't just about technical tricks; it's a mindset shift. Be mindful of the information you share on your phone, practice good app hygiene, and remember that true anonymity requires vigilance and responsible digital habits.

With the tools and tips in this chapter, you're now equipped to transform your mobile device from a surveillance tool into a vessel of digital freedom. So, raise your anonymized sails, intrepid voyager, and chart your course towards a more private and secure mobile experience. Remember, the road less traveled, shrouded in the shadows of anonymity, awaits your exploration.

From understanding hidden networks to securing your communications and browsing anonymously, you're now empowered to reclaim your digital freedom and privacy in the ever-evolving landscape of the online world. Remember, knowledge is your shield, caution is your compass, and responsibility is your torch. Embrace the shadows, wield your tools wisely, and continue your exploration of the hidden corners of the internet where your true voice can still be heard, loud and clear, within the hushed chambers of digital privacy.

Now, go forth and explore with confidence, leaving only the faintest footprints in the sands of cyberspace. The Darknet, with all its potential and perils, awaits.

Chapter 8:

Encryption: The Ultimate Shield

In a world where information is currency, encryption stands as the ultimate shield, guarding your secrets against prying eyes and malicious forces. This chapter delves into the art of digital alchemy, revealing how encryption transforms ordinary data into unintelligible ciphers, protecting your privacy and securing your communications. We'll explore the inner workings of encryption, unravel the mysteries of different algorithms, and equip you with the knowledge to forge your own impenetrable fortress in the digital realm.

The Magical Cipher: Transforming Data into Puzzles

Imagine a language so intricate, so complex, that only those with the right key can decipher its meaning. That's the essence of encryption. It takes your sensitive data—messages, files, passwords—and scrambles it using mathematical algorithms, rendering it unreadable to anyone without the decryption key.

The Key Keepers: Symmetric and Asymmetric Encryption

Encryption's magic relies on two distinct guardians of the keys:

- Symmetric Encryption: Like a secret handshake, both parties use the same key to encrypt and decrypt data. It's fast and efficient, but sharing the key securely can be challenging.

  o Common Algorithms: AES (Advanced Encryption Standard), Blowfish, Twofish.

- Asymmetric Encryption: A dance of two keys—a public key shared openly, and a private key kept hidden. Anyone can encrypt with the public key, but only the holder of the private key can decrypt, ensuring secure communication without prior key exchange.

- Common Algorithms: RSA (Rivest-Shamir-Adleman), ECC (Elliptic Curve Cryptography).

Strength in Diversity: Cipher Suites and Hashing

Encryption's power grows when combined with other techniques:

- Cipher Suites: Bundles of algorithms and protocols working in harmony to secure different aspects of communication, ensuring confidentiality, integrity, and authentication.

- Hashing: A one-way encryption that creates unique fingerprints of data, used for password storage, file integrity checks, and digital signatures.

- ○ Common Hashing Algorithms: SHA-256, SHA-3, MD5.

Choosing Your Armor: Strengths and Weaknesses of Algorithms

Each algorithm has its unique strengths and potential vulnerabilities:

- AES: The gold standard for symmetric encryption, known for its speed and resilience against attacks.

- RSA: A widely used asymmetric algorithm, but its security depends on key length and proper implementation.

- ECC: A newer asymmetric algorithm offering stronger security with smaller keys, making it ideal for resource-constrained devices.

Beyond the Technical: Encryption in Action

Encryption isn't just for spies and hackers; it's woven into the fabric of our digital lives:

- Securing Online Transactions: HTTPS protects your financial data and passwords when shopping or banking online.

- Protecting Personal Communications: Secure messaging apps like Signal and WhatsApp employ end-to-end encryption to safeguard your conversations.

- Safeguarding Data Storage: Encrypting files and devices protects sensitive information from unauthorized access.

Wielding the Cipher: Tips for Everyday Encryption

Here are ways to integrate encryption into your digital life:

- Use password managers: Store and manage passwords securely with tools like LastPass or 1Password.

- Enable encryption on devices: Protect your smartphones and laptops with encryption features.

- Choose encrypted messaging apps: Opt for apps with strong encryption protocols for communication.

- Encrypt sensitive files: Use tools like VeraCrypt or PGP to protect important documents.

- Be mindful of key management: Protect your decryption keys securely, as losing them means losing access to your encrypted data.

Embracing the Cipher's Power: A Call to Action

In a world increasingly reliant on data, encryption is not a luxury; it's a necessity. By understanding its fundamentals and applying its tools wisely, you can forge a fortress of privacy and security in the digital realm. Remember, knowledge is your shield, and encryption is your sword. Wield them both with care, and navigate the digital landscape with confidence, knowing that your secrets are safe within the embrace of the cipher.

Chapter 9:

Coin Mixing: Breaking the Trace

Welcome, fellow crypto enthusiast, to the labyrinthine world of coin mixing! In this chapter, we'll unravel the mysteries of this powerful tool used to anonymize cryptocurrency transactions, shedding light on its workings and empowering you to make informed decisions about its use.

The Problem: Transparent Trails on the Blockchain

Imagine every step you take with your cryptocurrency etched in stone, visible to anyone with a magnifying glass. That's the inherent transparency of the blockchain, offering security but sacrificing anonymity. Every transaction, from sender to receiver and beyond, is laid bare for all to see. This exposes users to potential risks like:

- Tracking and Surveillance: Your spending habits and financial connections can be analyzed by anyone, raising privacy concerns.

- Targeted Attacks: Hackers or malicious actors could potentially target your crypto holdings based on your transaction history.

- Price Manipulation: Large transactions can become visible, potentially influencing market prices and affecting your trades.

Enter the Coin Mixer: Breaking the Chains of Transparency

Coin mixing, also known as crypto tumbling, works like a magical laundry machine for your dirty crypto coins. It takes your crypto, throws it into a swirling pool with other users' coins, and then distributes a clean (and hopefully untraceable) portion back to you. Here's a simplified breakdown:

1. Deposit your coins: You send your cryptocurrency to a mixing service.

2. Coin Pool Formation: The service combines your coins with those from other users, creating a large pool.

3. Mixing Magic: The service employs various techniques to shuffle and anonymize the coins within the pool. Common methods include:

   o Chain splitting: Breaking down coins into smaller denominations and sending them through different paths on the blockchain.

   o Coin swapping: Exchanging coins between pool participants, obscuring the original transaction trail.

- Delayed transactions: Scheduling payouts at random intervals to further break the link between deposits and withdrawals.

4. Withdrawal: You receive your "clean" coins back (minus a mixing fee) from a different address, ideally with no link back to your original deposit.

Unmasking the Risks and Limitations: Before You Take the Plunge

While coin mixing offers substantial anonymity benefits, it's crucial to understand its limitations and potential risks:

- Not Foolproof: Mixing services can't guarantee complete anonymity. Advanced blockchain analysis techniques might still trace some connections.

- Centralization Concerns: Relying on a third-party mixing service introduces trust issues. Choose reputable services with strong security practices.

- Transaction Delays: Mixing processes can take time, leading to delayed withdrawals and potential inconvenience.

- Legality Issues: Some jurisdictions view coin mixing with suspicion due to its association with illegal activities. Research local regulations before engaging in such services.

Taking the First Steps: A Beginner's Guide to Coin Mixing

If you're intrigued by the potential of coin mixing, here are some helpful starting points:

- Research mixing services: Look for reputable services with good reviews and strong security protocols. Check features like supported currencies, mixing algorithms, and fees.

- Start small: Don't jump into mixing large amounts right away. Experiment with small transactions to understand the process and assess the service's effectiveness.

- Practice caution: Use a secure VPN to mask your internet activity and always choose reliable wallets for storing your mixed coins.

- Stay informed: Keep up with the latest developments in blockchain analysis and privacy techniques to understand evolving risks and adjust your approach accordingly.

Beyond the Mix: A Call to Responsible Digital Citizenship

Coin mixing is a powerful tool, but it's not a magic bullet for absolute anonymity. Remember, responsible digital citizenship requires a holistic approach to privacy and security. Combine mixing with other best practices like secure password management, strong encryption, and mindful online behavior to maximize your anonymity and safeguard your crypto holdings.

Here are some helpful resources to expand on the information in Chapter 9:

Coin Mixing Services:

- Wasabi Wallet: https://cryptobriefing.com/wasabis-bitcoin-mixer-to-start-censoring-transactions/ (Provides detailed information about coin mixing and offers a user-friendly wallet with built-in mixing functionalities.)

- Blender.io: https://blendor.io/ (A popular mixing service with a focus on transparency and detailed statistics.)

- CoinJoin: https://blog.wasabiwallet.io/what-is-a-coinjoin/ (An open-source coin mixing software that allows users to mix their coins directly, without relying on a third-party service.)

Step-by-step Guides:

- How to Use Wasabi Wallet: https://cryptobriefing.com/wasabis-bitcoin-mixer-to-start-censoring-transactions/ (A comprehensive guide explaining how to use Wasabi Wallet for mixing Bitcoin.)

- Coin Mixing for Beginners: https://news.bitcoin.com/tumbling-bitcoins-guide-rinse-cycle/ (Provides a basic overview of coin mixing and walks you through the process using a specific service.)

- Understanding Coin Mixing: https://medium.com/thedarkside/top-10-bitcoin-mixers-and-bitcoin-tumbler-services-review-2020-1524445bf86d (Offers a technical explanation of the different coin mixing algorithms and their effectiveness.)

Additional Resources:

- Bitcoin Magazine: https://bitcoinmagazine.com/ (Provides news and information about Bitcoin and other cryptocurrencies, including articles on coin mixing and privacy.)

- Privacy Tools & Services Directory: https://www.privacytools.io/ (A comprehensive directory of tools and resources for online privacy, including coin mixing services.)

- Electronic Frontier Foundation (EFF): https://www.eff.org/ (Provides information and resources on internet privacy and digital rights, including the use of encryption and anonymity tools.)

Important Note:

Before using any coin mixing service, it's crucial to research them thoroughly. Consider factors like their reputation, security practices, supported currencies, fees, and potential legal implications in your jurisdiction. Remember, coin mixing is not a guarantee of complete anonymity, and it's essential to use it responsibly and with caution.

By using these resources and practicing responsible digital citizenship, you can gain a deeper understanding of coin mixing and make informed decisions about whether it's the right tool for your needs.

Embrace the knowledge you've gained in this chapter, and venture into the world of coin mixing with caution and understanding. Remember, anonymity is a journey, not a destination. Continue exploring, learning, and evolving your digital hygiene practices to navigate the blockchain with confidence and control, leaving only the faintest footprints in your wake.

Now go forth, mix with mindful wisdom, and enjoy the enhanced privacy and security that awaits!

Chapter 10:

Anonymity for the Truly Paranoid

Welcome, fellow traveler in the labyrinthine alleys of digital anonymity. This chapter delves into the deepest shadows, catering to those whose pursuit of privacy transcends ordinary measures. We journey into the realm of advanced anonymity techniques, reserved for those with a heightened level of paranoia and a thirst for the most impregnable digital cloaks. Prepare to encounter intricate enclaves, enigmatic proofs, and a kaleidoscope of tools designed to vanish you utterly from the prying eyes of the cybernetic panopticon.

Fortress of Solitude: Secure Enclaves for the Impenetrable

Imagine a digital sanctuary, a space carved from the bedrock of the internet, accessible only through layers of impenetrable encryption and guarded by vigilant sentinels. Such is the domain of secure enclaves, fortified environments where you can conduct your digital machinations unseen, unheard, and untraceable. These havens utilize a cocktail of technologies, including:

- Hardware enclaves: Secure chips embedded within your device, acting as isolated fortresses for sensitive operations. Think of them as miniature, inviolable vaults within your digital walls.

- Trusted Execution Environments (TEEs): Secure virtualized spaces within your operating system, shielding your activities from the prying eyes of the main system. Imagine a hidden room within your digital house, accessible only through a secret passage.

- Secure multi-party computation (MPC): A collaborative approach where computations are distributed among multiple servers, with individual parties contributing only their inputs without ever having access to the complete picture. Think of a puzzle solved by blindfolded participants, each holding a piece, with the final image revealed only to the collective effort.

Beyond the Veil: Zero-Knowledge Proofs for Invisible Transactions

Imagine proving you know something without revealing what it is. That's the magic of zero-knowledge proofs, cryptographic tools that allow you to verify an assertion (say, owning a certain asset) without disclosing any identifying information. Think of it as unlocking a door by demonstrating your knowledge of the combination without anyone ever seeing the numbers themselves. These ethereal proofs serve as digital passports, granting access to services and resources without leaving a trace of your identity.

Navigating the Labyrinth: Tools for the Advanced Paranoid

Your toolbox for hyper-anonymity extends far beyond the usual suspects. Here are some potent tools for the truly cautious:

- Tails/Whonix: Specialized operating systems designed for anonymity and security, with features like Tor integration and persistent amnesiac browsing.

- Verifiable Random Functions (VRFs): Tools that generate unpredictable, verifiable randomness, ideal for anonymizing your interactions with blockchain networks.

- Homomorphic encryption: Allows computations to be performed on encrypted data without decryption, preserving privacy while utilizing data's full potential. Imagine a locked box where calculations happen inside, revealing only the results, not the contents.

- Secure multi-party communication (MPC): Enables confidential communication between multiple parties without any individual party having access to the entire conversation. Think of a group chat where everyone whispers, and only the collective meaning emerges.

A Call to Measured Paranoia: Security without Sacrifice

While your paranoia may be justified in these hyper-connected times, remember that absolute anonymity comes at a cost. Consider these trade-offs:

- Complexity: Advanced tools often require technical expertise and specialized knowledge, creating a steep learning curve.

- Availability: Some technologies are still in their infancy, offering limited functionality or compatibility.

- Convenience: Sacrificing ease of use and speed for enhanced anonymity can impact your daily workflow.

Embrace a measured paranoia, choosing solutions that strike the right balance between security and practicality. Layer your defenses strategically, prioritizing the threats you face most acutely. Remember, knowledge is your shield, and vigilance is your compass. Use them wisely as you navigate the shadowy alleys of this chapter, emerging equipped to vanish into the digital ether, a ghost amidst the machines.

This concludes our comprehensive exploration of anonymity in the digital age. From understanding hidden networks to securing your communications and employing advanced techniques, you are now empowered to reclaim your privacy and navigate the online world with confidence. Remember, knowledge is your shield, caution is your compass, and responsibility is your torch. Embrace the shadows, wield your tools with wisdom, and continue your exploration of the hidden corners of the internet where your true voice can still be heard, loud and clear, within the hushed chambers of digital privacy.

Now, go forth, vanish into the ether, and leave only the faintest whispers in your wake. The shadows await, and the truly paranoid shall always find their way.

To further enhance your exploration of advanced anonymity techniques, here are some helpful resources for each section of Chapter 10:

Secure Enclaves:

- Intel
  SGX: https://www.intel.com/content/w

ww/us/en/download/19085/intel-
software-guard-extensions-intel-sgx-
driver-for-windows.html (Official Intel
SGX website, with technical details and
resources)

- AMD
  SEV: https://www.amd.com/en/develop
  er/sev.html (Official AMD SEV
  website, with technical details and
  resources)

- Trusted Execution Environment (TEE)
  Alliance: https://www.securetechallianc
  e.org/wp-content/uploads/TEE-101-
  White-Paper-V1.1-FINAL-June-
  2018.pdf (Industry consortium
  promoting TEE adoption, with
  educational resources and member
  companies)

Zero-Knowledge Proofs:

- Zero-Knowledge Proofs
  101: https://crypto.stanford.edu/cs355/

18sp/lec3.pdf (Stanford Computer Science Department's introductory article on ZKPs)

- Zcash: https://z.cash/ (Privacy-focused cryptocurrency utilizing ZKPs)

- zkSNARKs: https://blog.ethereum.org/2016/12/05/zksnarks-in-a-nutshell (Open-source library for building and verifying zkSNARK proofs)

Advanced Paranoia Toolbox:

- Tails: https://tails.net/support/faq/index.en.html (Amnesiac Linux distribution for secure browsing and anonymity)

- Whonix: https://www.whonix.org/ (Virtual machine distribution focused on online anonymity and security)

- Verifiable Random Functions (VRFs): https://en.wikipedia.org/wiki/Verifiable_random_function (Wikipedia article on VRFs, with technical details and research papers)

- Homomorphic Encryption: https://en.wikipedia.org/wiki/Homomorphic_encryption (Wikipedia article on homomorphic encryption, with technical details and examples)

- Secure Multi-Party Computation (MPC): https://en.wikipedia.org/wiki/Secure_multi-party_computation (Wikipedia article on MPC, with technical details and research papers)

Additional Resources:

- The Privacy Tools & Services Directory: https://www.privacytools.io/ (Comprehensive directory of tools and resources for online privacy)

- The Electronic Frontier Foundation (EFF): https://www.eff.org/ (Non-profit organization promoting digital rights and privacy, with resources and research)

- Books:

  - "The Paranoiac's Guide to Hiding" by Edward Snowden and Bruce Schneier

  - "Zero-Knowledge Proofs: An Introduction" by Ariel Rubinstein and Asaf Rabinowitz

Remember: Implementing advanced anonymity techniques often requires technical expertise and careful consideration of trade-offs. Use these resources responsibly and prioritize solutions that align with your specific needs and threat landscape.

I hope these links provide a valuable starting point for your continued journey into the shadows!

Chapter 11:

The Battle for Privacy: Governments vs. Big Tech

Welcome to the battleground of the 21st century - the battleground for privacy. In this arena, two titans clash: governments, wielding the sword of public safety and national security, and Big Tech, armed with the potent arsenal of data and innovation. This chapter delves into the heart of this ongoing conflict, exploring its origins, consequences, and the potential game-changers on the horizon, like blockchain and artificial intelligence.

The Genesis of the Clash: A Landscape of Data Collection

Our digital lives generate a constant stream of data - our every click, swipe, and purchase meticulously recorded by the omnipresent eyes of the internet. This trove of information has become the lifeblood of Big Tech, enabling targeted advertising, personalized experiences, and powerful algorithms that predict and influence our behavior. However, governments perceive this data collection as a double-edged sword. While it facilitates crime prevention and intelligence gathering, it also raises concerns about:

- Mass Surveillance: The potential for governments to abuse their access to personal data and erode individual liberties.

- Data Breaches: The vulnerability of vast data ecosystems to hacking and leaks, exposing sensitive information to malicious actors.

- Algorithmic Bias: The possibility of biased algorithms perpetuating discrimination and unfairness in areas like law enforcement and loan approvals.

The Skirmish Lines: Encryption, Data Localization, and Right to be Forgotten

Governments have launched various offensives to protect their citizens' privacy and curb Big Tech's data dominion. Some key battlegrounds include:

- Encryption: Governments seeking backdoors to bypass encryption used by messaging apps and other platforms, sparking fierce debates about security and privacy trade-offs.

- Data Localization: Laws mandating local storage of user data within national borders, giving governments greater control but potentially hindering global businesses.

- Right to be Forgotten: Regulations granting individuals the right to request deletion of their personal data from search engines and online platforms, challenging Big Tech's data retention practices.

The New Frontiers: Blockchain and AI Redefining the Battlefield

Emerging technologies like blockchain and artificial intelligence have the potential to reshape the privacy landscape:

- Blockchain: With its decentralized data storage and tamper-proof nature, blockchain offers an alternative to centralized Big Tech databases, potentially empowering individuals to reclaim control over their data.

- AI: Privacy-preserving AI algorithms are being developed to enable data analysis without compromising individual privacy, potentially offering a solution to the tension between data utilization and citizen protection.

The Uncertain Future: Navigating the Digital Minefield

The outcome of this epic battle for privacy remains uncertain. Governments face the pressure of balancing security with individual rights, while Big Tech must navigate the ethical tightrope of innovation and data responsibility. As new technologies emerge, the landscape will only become more complex.

A Call for Collaborative Defense: Citizens as the Ultimate Weapon

Amidst this clash, one key factor remains constant: the voice of the citizens. We, the data producers, must actively engage in this crucial battle. By demanding transparency, advocating for strong privacy laws, and embracing technologies that empower us, we can become the ultimate defense in this digital minefield.

Remember, our privacy is not a privilege, but a fundamental right. Let us raise our voices, wield our knowledge, and fight for a future where technology serves humanity, not exploits it, where the digital world respects the boundaries of our private lives, and where the echo of our footsteps in the online sand fades, leaving only the whispers of individual freedom.

The battle for privacy is far from over. This chapter is just the beginning of a crucial conversation. Together, we can ensure that technology becomes a tool for empowerment, not a weapon of surveillance, and that the shadows of the digital age become not a place of fear, but a refuge for our most precious possession: our right to be unseen, unheard, and utterly ourselves.

Now, go forth, raise your digital shields, and join the fight for a world where privacy reigns supreme.

Government vs. Big Tech: Battle Scars in the Digital Arena

The fight for privacy in the digital age is a clash of titans, with governments wielding the shield of public safety and Big Tech brandishing the sword of innovation, all while citizens stand in the crossfire. This chapter delves into the trenches of this ongoing war, showcasing key battles that have shaped the landscape and highlighting the impact on our digital lives.

1. Facebook's Cambridge Analytica Scandal: In 2018, it was revealed that the personal data of millions of Facebook users had been improperly accessed and used for targeted political advertising by Cambridge Analytica. This case ignited global outrage, raising concerns about data privacy, political manipulation, and the power of social media giants.

Impact: Stricter data protection laws emerged, like the EU's General Data Protection Regulation (GDPR), giving users more control over their data and imposing hefty fines on companies for privacy breaches. Social media platforms faced increased scrutiny and pressure to be more transparent with data practices.

2. Google's Antitrust Battles: Since 2020, Google has been embroiled in antitrust lawsuits filed by the US Department of Justice and multiple states, alleging the company uses its dominant search engine position to stifle competition and harm consumers. Similar investigations are ongoing in Europe.

Impact: Potential changes to search engine algorithms and how online advertising is conducted could arise. Smaller businesses might benefit from a more level playing field in the online marketplace. Consumers may see more diverse search results and potentially lower prices for online services.

3. YouTube's Content Moderation Conundrum: As a platform brimming with user-generated content, YouTube faces the

constant challenge of balancing freedom of expression with content moderation. Governments worldwide have pressured the platform to remove videos deemed extremist, hateful, or harmful.

Impact: Stricter content moderation policies can lead to censorship concerns and the removal of legitimate viewpoints. Balancing free speech with harmful content remains a delicate dance, impacting what users see and how they engage with information online.

4. The Great Firewall of China: China's extensive internet censorship apparatus, popularly known as the Great Firewall, restricts access to foreign websites and social media platforms like Facebook and Google. This raises concerns about government control of information and limits access to diverse perspectives for Chinese citizens.

Impact: Limited access to global information can hinder educational and economic opportunities for individuals within China. It also raises concerns about the role of governments in shaping online discourse and suppressing dissent.

5. The Rise of Data Localization Laws: Several countries, including India and Russia, have implemented data localization laws, requiring technology companies to store user data within their borders. This raises concerns about government access to data and potential barriers to global businesses.

Impact: Data localization can increase costs for companies and potentially hinder innovation. It can also restrict data flow and limit access to international services for users in certain countries.

These are just a few examples of the ongoing battle between governments and Big Tech. Each case has far-reaching consequences, impacting how we access information, engage with online platforms, and interact with the digital world. As citizens, it's crucial to stay informed about these developments, understand their implications, and advocate for policies that protect our privacy and promote a free and open internet.

Remember, the digital battlefield is ever-evolving, and our role in shaping its future is vital. By raising our voices, demanding transparency, and supporting solutions that empower individuals, we can navigate the labyrinthine paths of online privacy and emerge on the other side, not as passive data points, but as informed citizens in control of our digital destinies.

Let us march forward, armed with knowledge and vigilance, towards a future where technology serves humanity, not exploits it, and where our digital footprints fade into the shadows, leaving only the echo of our voices demanding a world where privacy reigns supreme.

A Guide to Anonymity in the Big Tech Era

Navigating the digital landscape dominated by Big Tech giants can feel like traversing a minefield. But fear not, for there are ways to safeguard yourself and claim a semblance of anonymity in this data-hungry ecosystem. Here are a few key tactics:

1. Mind Your Data Footprint:

- Minimize data sharing: Be mindful of what information you share on social media and other platforms. Consider using alternative platforms with stronger privacy policies.

- Regularly review privacy settings: Take control of your privacy settings on all platforms you use. Opt out of data sharing wherever possible and limit the information accessible to others.

- Practice digital minimalism: Reduce your online presence by deleting old accounts and content you no longer use. The less data you have out there, the less vulnerable you are.

2. Embrace Encryption:

- Encrypt your communications: Use encrypted messaging apps like Signal or Telegram for private conversations. Consider encrypting your emails and files as well.

- Use a VPN: Virtual Private Networks anonymize your online activity by masking your IP address and encrypting your internet traffic. Choose reputable VPN providers with strong security practices.

3. Be Browser Smart:

- Use a privacy-focused browser: Switch from mainstream browsers like Chrome or Safari to options like DuckDuckGoGo or Brave, which prioritize user privacy and offer built-in tracking protection.

- Install privacy extensions: Add browser extensions like uBlock Origin and Privacy Badger to block trackers and intrusive ads, further minimizing your data footprint.

4. Seek Alternatives:

- Support smaller, privacy-focused platforms: Explore alternatives to popular Big Tech services. Opt for decentralized search engines like DuckDuckGo and cloud storage solutions like Mega for a more private experience.

- Use open-source software: Open-source software offers greater transparency and often prioritizes user privacy over proprietary tools. Consider open-source alternatives for your daily needs.

5. Stay Informed:

- Follow news and updates on data privacy issues: Arm yourself with knowledge about the latest threats and developments in the fight for online privacy.

- Support organizations advocating for digital rights: Join forces with organizations fighting for stronger data protection laws and user privacy.

Remember, absolute anonymity online is difficult, but taking these steps can significantly reduce your data footprint and make it harder for Big Tech companies to track and exploit your information. By adopting a layered approach and remaining vigilant, you can reclaim some control over your digital life and navigate the online world with a greater sense of privacy and security.

So, raise your digital shields, wield your knowledge as your weapon, and march forward toward a future where you control your own data and own your place in the digital landscape.

Chapter 12:

Taking Back Your Privacy: A Call to Action

The battle for privacy is not a passive spectator sport. It's a daily battle fought on the keyboards, in the code, and in the halls of power. In this final chapter, we cast off the cloak of the observer and rise as active participants, armed with knowledge and empowered with actionable steps to reclaim our digital sovereignty.

Empowering Yourself: Daily Hacks for Digital Defense

The first line of defense lies in your own hands. Take these steps to fortify your digital walls:

- Audit your digital footprint: Review your social media

accounts, subscriptions, and online presence. Purge unused accounts, remove unnecessary permissions, and tighten privacy settings across all platforms.

- Embrace encrypted communication: Use encrypted messaging apps, email encryption tools, and VPNs to shield your online conversations and activities.

- Browse like a ghost: Opt for privacy-focused browsers like DuckDuckGoGo and Brave, and employ browser extensions like uBlock Origin and Privacy Badger to block trackers and invasive ads.

- Become a password ninja: Ditch easily guessable passwords, embrace password managers, and enable two-factor authentication wherever possible.

- Think before you click: Be wary of phishing scams and suspicious links. Be mindful of what information you share online, and avoid oversharing sensitive data.

Building a Collective Fortress: Joining the Privacy Rebellion

Individual actions are powerful, but collective efforts resonate like thunder. Join the privacy revolution by:

- Supporting privacy-focused organizations: Lend your voice and resources to organizations fighting for stronger data protection laws and advocating for user privacy.

- Demanding ethical technology: Voice your concerns to tech companies, government officials, and elected representatives about privacy-invasive practices and demand ethical data usage.

- Educate and empower others: Share your knowledge with friends, family, and colleagues. Help them understand the importance of online privacy and equip them with tools to protect themselves.

- Vote with your clicks: Choose privacy-friendly alternatives to Big Tech services. Support platforms that prioritize user privacy and respect your data.

- Stay informed: Follow news and updates on data privacy issues, emerging threats, and legislative developments.

Beyond the Battlefield: Cultivating a Privacy Mindset

Remember, privacy is not just about technological tools and legislative battles. It's a mindset, a value woven into the fabric of our digital lives. Cultivate a culture of privacy by:

- Practicing mindful online conduct: Be conscious of what you share and where you share it. Remember, the internet is a permanent archive, and once released, digital whispers can carry far.

- Valuing your data as an asset: Your personal information is valuable, not a commodity to be freely traded.

- Demanding transparency and accountability: Hold tech companies and governments responsible for their data practices. Demand clear explanations, transparent policies, and meaningful consequences for privacy violations.

A Future Woven with Privacy Threads

The path to reclaiming our online privacy is not easy, but it is paved with the footsteps of countless digital warriors who came before us. Remember, every conscious click, every encrypted message, every voice raised in defense of privacy, contributes to a future where technology empowers, not exploits, where our digital shadows fade gracefully, and where we stand tall, not as data points, but as individuals in control of our own narrative.

So, raise your banner, digital citizen, and join the fight. Let the echoes of our collective demand for privacy resonate through the corridors of power and the silicon valleys. Let us weave a future where technology serves as a tool for freedom, not a weapon of control, and where our right to digital self-determination shines bright in the shadows of the internet.

The battle for privacy is far from over, but within each of us lies the power to rewrite the narrative. Let us be the authors of a future where privacy reigns supreme, and where the whispers of our digital lives fade into the ether, carrying the echoes of a victory hard-won, but well-deserved.

Go forth, digital warrior, and fight for the future of privacy. The shadows await, but so does the dawn of a new era, where you, too, can become a legend in the fight for the most precious right of all - the right to be unseen, unheard, and utterly yourself.

www.ingramcontent.com/pod-product-compliance
Lightning Source LLC
LaVergne TN
LVHW051742050326
832903LV00029B/2667

* 9   7   9   8   8   7   3   7   7   2   9   8   8 *